W9-BVX-403

DATE DUE

1019
020

DISCARD

Hudson Area Public Library
Hudson, IL 61748

MIGHTY MACHINES

Monster Trucks

by Kay Manolis

Hudson Area Public Library
Hudson, IL 61748

BELLWETHER MEDIA · MINNEAPOLIS, MN

BLASTOFF!
READERS

Note to Librarians, Teachers, and Parents:

Blastoff! Readers are carefully developed by literacy experts and combine standards-based content with developmentally appropriate text.

Level 1 provides the most support through repetition of high-frequency words, light text, predictable sentence patterns, and strong visual support.

Level 2 offers early readers a bit more challenge through varied simple sentences, increased text load, and less repetition of high-frequency words.

Level 3 advances early-fluent readers toward fluency through increased text and concept load, less reliance on visuals, longer sentences, and more literary language.

Level 4 builds reading stamina by providing more text per page, increased use of punctuation, greater variation in sentence patterns, and increasingly challenging vocabulary.

Level 5 encourages children to move from "learning to read" to "reading to learn" by providing even more text, varied writing styles, and less familiar topics.

Whichever book is right for your reader, Blastoff! Readers are the perfect books to build confidence and encourage a love of reading that will last a lifetime!

This edition first published in 2008 by Bellwether Media, Inc.

No part of this publication may be reproduced in whole or in part without written permission of the publisher. For information regarding permission, write to Bellwether Media, Inc., Attention: Permissions Department, 5357 Penn Avenue South, Minneapolis, MN 55419.

Library of Congress Cataloging-in-Publication Data
Manolis, Kay.
  Monster trucks / by Kay Manolis.
    p. cm. – (Blastoff! readers. Mighty machines)
Summary: "Simple text and full-color photographs introduce young readers to monster trucks. Intended for students in kindergarten through third grade"–Provided by publisher.
  Includes bibliographical references and index.
  ISBN 978-1-60014-178-2 (hardcover : alk. paper)
  1. Monster trucks–Juvenile literature. I. Title.
  TL230.15.M36 2008
  629.224–dc22
                                                    2007040554

Text copyright © 2008 by Bellwether Media, Inc. BLASTOFF! READERS and associated logos are trademarks and/or registered trademarks of Bellwether Media, Inc. SCHOLASTIC, CHILDREN'S PRESS, and associated logos are trademarks and/or registered trademarks of Scholastic Inc.

Printed in the United States of America, North Mankato, MN.   110110   1178

Contents

RUMBLE! ROAR!
Here comes
a monster truck!
Monster trucks
are **pickup**
trucks with
huge tires.

Some monster truck tires are taller than you!

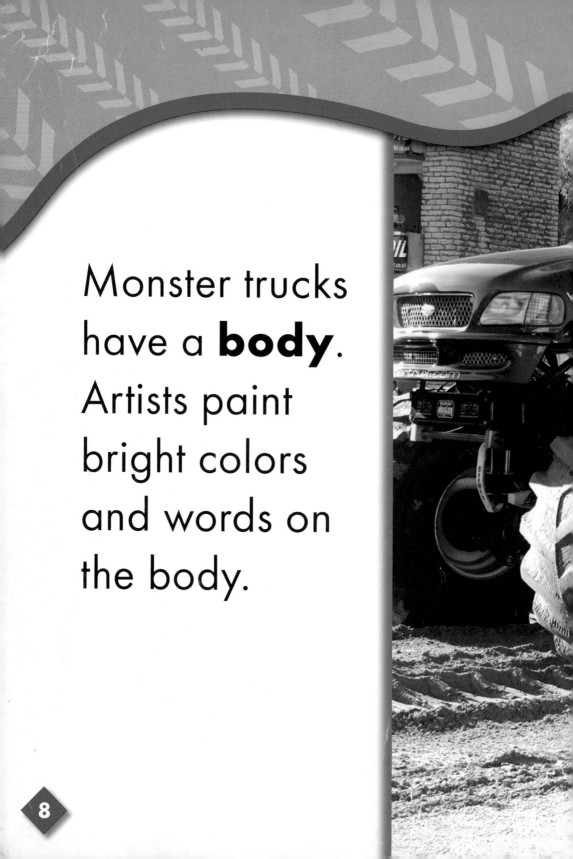

Monster trucks have a **body**. Artists paint bright colors and words on the body.

Most monster trucks have their name painted on their body. This one is named **Bigfoot**!

Monster trucks
have big
engines.
An engine
gives a truck
its power.

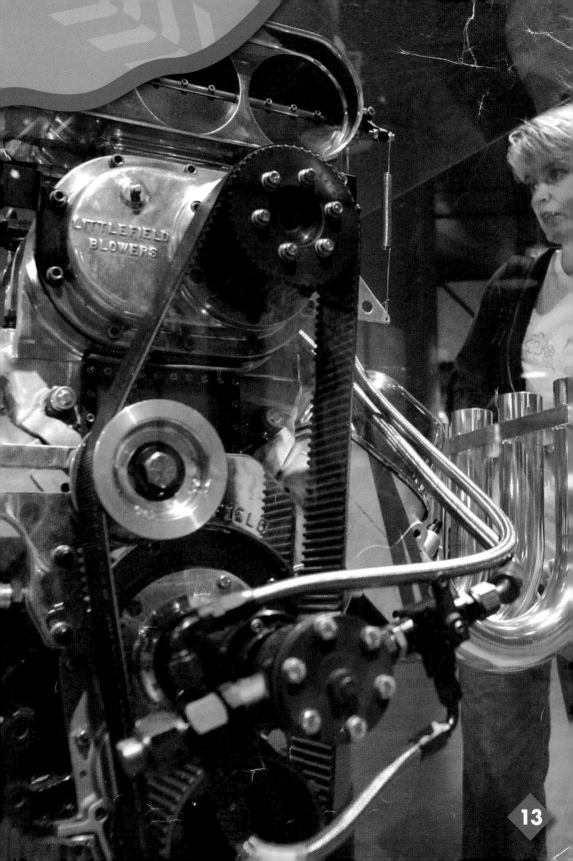

Monster trucks
can crush cars.

Monster trucks can also race around a **track**.

Sometimes monster trucks break apart. This black truck is losing some of its body.

19

Monster trucks
leap over cars.
This monster
truck leaps
4 white cars.

Glossary

Bigfoot—the very first monster truck ever built; Bigfoot was built in the 1970s by Bob Chandler.

body—the part of a vehicle that carries passengers; monster truck bodies usually have bright colors and designs.

engine—a machine that makes a vehicle move

pickup—a truck with an open body and low sides

track—an area made for racing

To Learn More

AT THE LIBRARY

Gould, Robert. *Monster Trucks*. Carlsbad, Calif.: Big Guy Books, 2004.

Nelson, Kristin L. *Monster Trucks*. Minneapolis, Minn.: Lerner, 2003.

Steele, Mark Anthony. *I'm a Great Big Monster Truck*. New York: Scholastic, 2004.

Todd, Mark. *Monster Trucks*. New York: Houghton Mifflin, 2003.

ON THE WEB

Learning more about mighty machines is as easy as 1, 2, 3.

1. Go to www.factsurfer.com

2. Enter "mighty machines" into search box.

3. Click the "Surf" button and you will see a list of related web sites.

With factsurfer.com, finding more information is just a click away.

Index

The images in this book are reproduced through the courtesy of: demonike, front cover; Peter Abrekstsen, p. 5; Barrett Stinson/Associated Press, Inc./Alamy, p. 7; Maksim Shmeljov, p. 9; Ian Dagnall/Alamy, p. 11; Anne Ryan/Associated Press, p. 13; Barry Salmons, p. 15; Maksim Shmeljov, p. 17; Jae C. Hong/Associated Press, p. 19; Barry Salmons, p. 21.

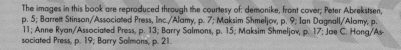